CONSIDERING CREATION

CONSIDERING CREATION

Examine the Evidence!

by
Bert Cargill

RITCHIE
John Ritchie Publishing

40 Beansburn, Kilmarnock, Scotland

ISBN-13: 978 1 912522 95 8

Copyright © 2020 by John Ritchie Ltd.
40 Beansburn, Kilmarnock, Scotland

www.ritchiechristianmedia.co.uk

Typeset by John Ritchie Ltd., Kilmarnock
Printed by Bell & Bain Ltd., Glasgow

Contents

Considering Creation

Preface

In asking you to consider creation, or nature as some people call it, I have to tell you that it has fascinated me for as long as I can remember. It's a long story, but I'll be brief just to put you in the picture. If you wish, you can skip this section!

An interest in Nature

My father was a fisherman and we lived in a house which overlooked a small tidal harbour. As a boy I became interested in the many birds I could see every day. One which intrigued me had long red legs and a long bill which it kept poking into the mud at the water's edge. I learned it was called a redshanks! Ever since then I've been interested in beautiful creatures like these wherever I've gone, walking for miles through forests and along coastlines, working on fishing boats on the North Sea, climbing some of the great Scottish mountains with my best friend or on my own, discovering such a variety of flora and fauna, gazing over such immense vistas. Travelling south of the equator into Africa, north to Iceland and Norway, across to the United States, and over to the Swiss, Italian and French Alps, opened up more stunning landscapes and seascapes to enjoy during the daytime, star-filled skies full of awe-inspiring wonder at night!

A deeper interest in Science

Science has enabled me to understand it all a bit more. My interest in science took root at secondary school, and was significantly deepened and widened during four enjoyable years at St Andrews University which awarded me a first class honours BSc in chemistry in 1962. After an industrial research job I became a lecturer at what is now Abertay University, Dundee where research into the solubility of gases in liquids led to my PhD in 1974. I continued my research at Abertay while lecturing on science degree courses until my retirement. Chemistry gave me a career and I enjoyed it.

An enduring interest in Christianity

Two other things have deeply impacted my life. The first of these is my Christian faith. I became a Christian in my early teens when I accepted Jesus Christ as my Saviour, believing that He had taken my sins away through His death on the cross. I've never forgotten it! Over many years in a changing world, Christ has been the solid rock of my faith. This faith was often challenged, not least by vigorous proponents of atheism and the theory of evolution - I could hardly miss this during my career! My honest assessment is that *from a scientific point of view* the foundations and claims of evolution are very questionable, and that creation by Almighty God is a logically sound and coherent basis for understanding the natural world. I have explored in detail both science and the Christian faith and found harmony and connections between them - not contradictions! This has been the subject of many lectures I have given to both sceptical and sympathetic audiences.

My family life

The other great influence in my life has been my stable family, both the one in which I grew up, and the one I presently enjoy. I have been married to Isobel, my best friend, for more than 50 years. Our two daughters and our son have between them given us six grandchildren and so far two great-grandchildren. They face a more confused and aggressively atheistic society than I did at their stage in life. This little book is dedicated to them all.

Bert Cargill, BSc, PhD
St Monans, Scotland
2020

Introduction

If work or lifestyle keeps you indoors most of the time, it does you good to get outside and take in the sights and sounds of the natural world.

Do you ever wonder about it, really *consider* how it all came to be as it is? All that beauty and variety? The many amazing creatures you can see every day? The flowers and trees you admire? The tiny insects all around you? The vast starry sky above you at night? All the regular changes you come to expect with the seasons? How day follows night, how tides ebb and flow, how weather patterns change and change the landscape?

There is a very popular story that all living things evolved from simpler ones by random processes involving chance mutations in their DNA and natural selection in the environment - with no foresight or design, and indeed from nothing to begin with! In this book I am challenging these ideas. I'm asking you to think seriously about creation, and about a Creator.

We never imagine that everything else around us has not been designed / made / created by someone - practical things we use and artistic things we admire. As for living things, our earliest intuition is that they too were created, and this is being reinforced nowadays by careful and detailed studies which show clear evidence of design. When you see a bird flying past your window, or a dog in the street, or a butterfly on a bush, the differences are clear, the design is obvious. Or look at the person next you! You don't immediately think that each evolved from a reptile or a fish or a worm, do you? You would never have imagined that if someone hadn't told you that story and kept insisting that's what happened!

When speaking about living things almost everyone calls them creatures. Should they now be called "evolutures"? The word "creatures" should keep reminding us that they really were created!

You can read these short chapters in any order. I'm beginning with incredibly small and basic things then going on to amazingly complex things, the living cells which make up every creature on earth. Next for your interest I'm describing in some detail a few of these fascinating creatures in their different habitats, and finally surveying unimaginably large things beyond earth's boundaries. Take this trip with me to examine the evidence for creation by design!

Enjoy the journey - here is the road map!

- Basic things and their intricacy
- Living things and their complexity
    - Birds and their beauty
    - Plants and their necessity
    - Insects and their society
    - The sea and its bounty
- The Universe and its immensity

1 Basic Things and their Intricacy

All around us, in the landscape and in the living world, huge variety and amazing beauty is everywhere. But everything we see is made from just a few basic substances called **elements**. About a hundred elements exist, and around three quarters of them are metals.

Elements combine with each other in specific ways to produce millions upon millions of different **compounds**. Thus, oxygen is an element, but combined with silicon and aluminium it is stone, combined with calcium and carbon it is chalk, combined with hydrogen it is water, combined with carbon and hydrogen it makes vitamin C, aspirin, wood, various plastics plus many, many other things.

The list of familiar materials is practically endless – paper and plastics, chalk and cheese, wood and stone, water and petrol, oxygen and methane, steel and copper, also vitamin C, aspirin, chlorophyll, insulin... Substances like these are made from only a few different elements. The commonest ones on earth are first oxygen, then silicon, aluminium and iron. Of special interest to us are the ones in living things – mostly carbon, hydrogen, nitrogen and oxygen. Of these, carbon is the key one with a unique ability to bond in many different ways to itself and to these other elements to give a huge number of substances called organic compounds.

Major Elements in the Earth's Crust

Oxygen (46.4%)   Silicon (28.2%)
Aluminium (8.3%)   Iron (5.6%)
Calcium (4.1%)   Sodium (2.4%)

Major Elements in the Human Body

Oxygen (65%)   Carbon (18%)
Hydrogen (10%) Nitrogen (3%)
Calcium (1.4%)   Phosphorus (1%)

If you took a piece of an element, say iron or copper, and split it up into smaller and smaller fragments until these were too small to see even with a powerful microscope, eventually we would get to the smallest particle of that element which could exist. It is called an **atom**, and it is *very* small. There are more than a billion billion atoms in the smallest fragment we could see, that is more than 1,000,000,000,000,000,000 atoms in that tiny speck of iron or copper! Yes, the atom is *very* small!

The atoms of any one element are all the same and are different in size and composition from the atoms of every other element. Small though they are, all atoms have a substructure. A nucleus at the centre contains positively charged **protons** and neutral **neutrons**[1], while other tiny negative particles called **electrons** whizz round this nucleus at near the speed of light in widely spaced orbits (or more precisely, orbitals).

---

[1]These particles have been shown to be aggregates of even smaller and more mysterious particles called quarks and leptons.

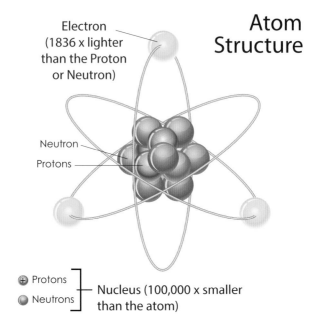

Electron
(1836 x lighter
than the Proton
or Neutron)

Atom Structure

Neutron

Protons

⊕ Protons
● Neutrons
Nucleus (100,000 x smaller than the atom)

Inside an atom there is a huge amount of empty space in which the electrons move, whereas in their nucleus the particles are very densely packed together and make up most of the mass of the atom. How all this came together in the first place is a real puzzle!

There is also energy locked in the atom, nuclear energy which, given the correct conditions, can be released. As you know this has great potential for damage and destruction as in a nuclear warhead, or harnessed for generating electricity. X-rays and radiotherapy are also derived from nuclear reactions. These have become great assets in the diagnosis and treatment of many diseases, although stringent control is necessary because excessive exposure can be lethal. Atomic structure is of great theoretical and practical interest.

The number of electrons at the outside of an atom decides if and how it can combine with other atoms. When this happens, we get **molecules** which are the smallest particles of compounds such as those described above. Molecules are therefore collections of atoms bonded to each other, sometimes just a few as in the case of water (H_2O) or carbon dioxide (CO_2) or methane (CH_4), sometimes in very large numbers as in chlorophyll or proteins or plastics (often called polymers).

An idea of how small all these particles are is indicated in *Fig 2*.

How small is small?

Water	Glucose	Antibody	Virus	Bacterium	Grain of Icing Sugar	Human Hair	Pencil Dot	Drawing Pin

10^{-1}	1	10	10^2	10^3	10^4	10^5	10^6	10^7

Nanometres (one thousand-millionth of a metre)
A 1mm pencil dot may contain more than 10^{20} atoms: that's 100,000,000,000,000,000,000 atoms! That same pencil dot could cover 10,000,000 (10^7) molecules of water. A 'big' molecule might measure only 1/100,000th (10^{-5}) of a millimetre but contain more than 10,000,000 (10^7) atoms.

Individual molecules have their own different 3-dimensional shapes and sizes, a fascinating "architecture" of their own. This is what gives the key properties to the substances concerned. A simple one like water is what it is because the H_2O molecule is not linear but bent as you can see in Fig 3, making it polar and enabling it to form reversible 'hydrogen-bonds' with its neighbours. For big molecules which enable living systems to function, such as proteins, enzymes, and notably DNA, each of their exact structures and shapes are critical. Minor changes in even one of their components would wreck the whole function. It looks as if they had been carefully designed for their job – more about this in the next chapter.

By far the most plentiful substance on earth is **water.** It is so common that we take it for granted and only miss it when it is unavailable. About 70% of the earth's surface is covered by water which is constantly being recycled, purified and redistributed. The heat of the sun evaporates it into the atmosphere from which it falls again in the form of rain, snow or dew, eventually to return to the sea[2]. It has been calculated that atmospheric water is changed and recycled about forty times per year.

The properties of water are remarkable, making it the only liquid which could support life. To do this it must be in liquid form, not solid ice or scalding steam. Here are some of these properties, all of which are predetermined by the shape of the H_2O molecule and its 'hydrogen-bonds' as we noted already.

- When water freezes, the solid is lighter than the liquid, and so ice floats on the surface. This becomes an insulating layer, preventing more freezing underneath and protecting aquatic life. Hardly any other substance has this property.

- Water is an efficient absorber of heat (has a high heat capacity), and so the large amount of water on earth acts as a beneficial buffer to temperature change as the seasons change, and also during day and night cycles. In the same way, the 55 – 65% water content of

---

[2]Long before science identified and understood this, it was described in the Bible - see Ecclesiastes 1.7.

our bodies keeps our temperatures steady, and if we need to cool down, evaporation of water (perspiration) is very effective.

- Water dissolves all kinds of substances. It carries nutrients to living cells and removes waste products along very narrow capillaries - its low viscosity and its high diffusion ability enables it to do this better than any other liquid could.

- Water absorbs much of the ultraviolet radiation which reaches our planet. This happens high in the atmosphere and on the surface of water bodies on earth, protecting living things from damage to their cells. Water also absorbs infrared which heats up the surface layer making it less dense than lower layers. It therefore remains at the top, preventing overheating and consequent loss of life-sustaining oxygen. But intriguingly, water is transparent to visible light which drives photosynthesis which continues well below the surface.

You can see how important and uniquely special water is!

What do you think ?

Scientists looking for evidence of life, look for water first. Water is the ideal (the only) fluid which can support life. The temperature at which it is a liquid exactly matches the temperature on earth which in turn is chiefly governed by the distance between earth and the sun. All an accident, do you think, or designed that way to support life on earth?

The forces between, and within, electrons, protons and neutrons are very precise. If these forces were even slightly different, atoms would not form and material substances could not exist. A detailed study of atomic and molecular structure would make you think that they were designed with the utmost precision to be the building blocks of everything.

Where did all the vast amount of material in the universe come from? Science says that matter cannot, of itself, be created or destroyed. It may be converted into energy according to Einstein's equation, $E = mc^2$, but energy cannot be created from nothing either. The existence of something rather than nothing, every item you see, points clearly to someone who made it. So wouldn't everything need a Creator who is outside of it all?

The universe had a beginning – it has not always existed. Science began to insist on this in the 1930s. The Bible said so thousands of years before: "In the beginning, God created the heavens and the earth" (Genesis 1.1). The popular idea is that it was a 'Big Bang', but natural causes and complex theories cannot explain what preceded that or caused it. Isn't almighty God the explanation? - with no chaotic Big Bang needed!

Don't accept the idea that the laws of science created everything – they describe what happens to things *after* they are there. Laws can't apply when nothing is there, and laws don't create anything.

2   Living Things and their Complexity

Life is a miracle and it is precious, easy to recognise and describe, but less easy to define in words. The difference between living and non-living things is obvious, and it is a fundamental law of science and an inescapable fact that life does not come from inanimate or dead matter. Living things die, but dead things do not become alive in the whole of the natural world. But what is life, and how did it begin?

The number and variety of living things on earth is immense. As we have seen, all are physically made up of only a few elements, the main ones being carbon, hydrogen, oxygen and nitrogen. It's how these elements combine to make different compounds that gives such huge variety everywhere. Their different molecules have unique three dimensional shapes which determine their specific functions. Along with others they make up amazingly complex structures called living cells which are the basic 'building blocks' of all forms of life.

The Living Cell

Our bodies contain about 100 million million of these cells which are continuously being renewed as others die off. On average they are about a hundredth of a millimetre in size. They used to be called 'simple cells', but not now! Biochemistry is revealing more and more of their astonishing, almost unfathomable complexity. They have more individual specialised components than a modern airliner or a supercomputer, all working together to do many things that these man-made structures cannot do – for example, they can repair themselves and create others like themselves! A fairly simplistic diagram of a cell is in Fig 1, and you may find that even that is complex enough!

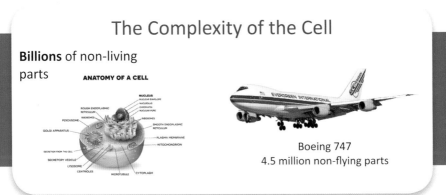

The Complexity of the Cell

Billions of non-living parts

ANATOMY OF A CELL

Boeing 747
4.5 million non-flying parts

A cell is like a miniature factory, operating according to specified instructions (the DNA which we will say more about shortly), using efficient transporters of energy and materials, to produce the substances required at the time. The most common of these substances are **proteins**, synthesised from their building blocks called **amino acids**, all fitting together according to a master plan. There are twenty different amino acids to choose from, which theoretically could make thousands of different proteins, but only one protein will have the correct size and shape of molecule for what the organism needs. The intricate processes in the cell (factory) select just the right amino acids in the right sequence to make the required protein, with no unfriendly by-products and no faulty goods! It does this continuously, making hundreds of different proteins all the time.

It's animal cells we are considering just now. We will look at plant cells later

- they have a few important differences. To describe all the components of a cell would take too long, so let's look at the innermost and the outermost parts - the nucleus with the DNA inside, and then the outer membrane (its 'skin').

DNA

The nucleus of the cell is its 'control centre' containing the instructions for the cell to function. These instructions are written in a code in a key substance called DNA (deoxyribonucleic acid). From Figure 2 you can see that the DNA molecule consists of two long spirals interconnected by specific cross-linkages made of pairs of four different amino acids. The ordering of these amino acids makes up the coded information which can be 'read' by another molecule called mRNA. This gives instructions to other components in the cell (the ribosomes) to manufacture whatever protein is required, and the original DNA is also copied.

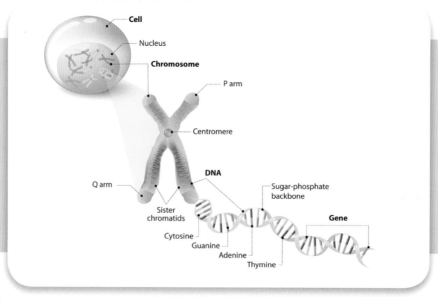

For us, instructions are usually written using letters of our alphabet, or sometimes drawings give instructions as in self-assembly packs for furniture.[1] For cells, the instructions are written using the four amino acids in the chemical code of DNA. The mRNA reads this and acts upon it. DNA therefore stores and transmits information which will specify all the features of a living creature, and it does so much more efficiently and compactly than any other known system. It has been calculated that the information in about a million million books could be stored in a sample of DNA the size of a pinhead! About 2 metres of this wonder substance is in the nucleus of our cells.

Each species of living creature has its own unique DNA. This makes it what it is, and copying enables it to reproduce offspring like itself. The DNA of one species cannot change into that of another species, because mechanisms in the cell ensure that when DNA is copied it is protected from change. However, in an effort to 'prove' evolution of species, it is often pointed out that 'mutations' (mistakes) may occur when DNA is copied. To test this idea in the laboratory, mutations have been induced in certain organisms. The results show these do not give anything useful or beneficial to the next generation but are harmful to the species. Not much hope of improving or changing a species by random mutations!

The Cell Membrane

A membrane is necessary to hold everything in place inside the cell – without it there would be no cell! It has to form a flexible 'skin' which is mechanically and chemically stable. It has to be insoluble in water, and

---

[1]A computer program uses 1s and 0s; Morse code or Braille uses dots and dashes or spaces; traffic lights use 3 colours – all provide information to the code-reader.

yet allow water-borne nutrients into the cell and also take waste products out. These vital transport processes take place by means of carefully designed protein channels[2] which go right through the membrane, while the membrane itself remains intact and waterproof. To manufacture all that would be a tall order for any system, but there it is, ready-made for these competing tasks - a marvel of intricate design!

Skip this next bit if it gets too complicated and take a look at Figure 3. But if you wish to know more about it, it is called a *phospholipid bilayer*. As the name suggests, it is built from two layers of lipids with their insoluble, long, fatty parts towards each other, back to back, while on the front surface of both layers, polar phosphate groups extend towards the inside and outside of the cell. These give affinity for the water around the cell and inside it.

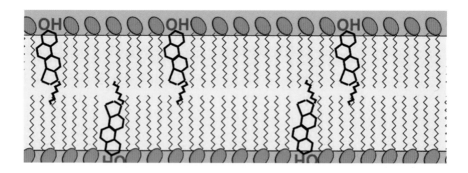

For a cell to be viable, everything it needs must be there from the beginning. The simplest cell you could imagine would never survive if some of its vital components were missing. The components themselves are so specialised

---

[2]They are called *aquaporins*,

and complex that random processes could never synthesise them to begin with! Successful manufacturing, today and any day, requires foresight, intelligent planning and design – chairs, clothing, cars, computers ... But not cells? - those much more marvellous living cells?

Statistically and logistically, unguided synthesis of even the smallest molecule which could replicate and might become a precursor of life is a non-starter.

- Statistically the calculations show it is well beyond finite probability.
- Logistically it is not feasible to get twenty amino acids together at once and select the right ones.
- Logically it is out of the question to get one of these functional proteins by accident or chance, and then join them up with others equally complex to make a living cell.

What do you think

There are serious obstacles in the way of gradual evolution of living things and, before that, of the single cells of which they are made. Here are some of these obstacles - overlooking or sidestepping them doesn't remove them!

1. The laws of chemistry show that it is impossible to synthesise from scratch even the simplest protein in the exact form required by living things. Besides, once present in the natural environment, such substances readily decompose and degrade. Forces of decomposition (sometimes called entropy) are always present to counteract synthesis – it is always much easier to slip back down a mountain than to climb up! That these proteins are there to

perform such intricate and efficient tasks, and that organisms are there to use them and maintain them, is truly remarkable. Could they arise simply by chance?

2. The Law of Biogenesis states that life cannot come from non-living material, only from living things already there. The gulf between non-living and living things cannot be ignored. So how did life begin, the greatest wonder of all?

3. There is also a huge gulf between invertibrates and vertibrates, and another real one between man and the 'cleverest' animal. The fossil records contain no traces of evolution's proposed intermediates – gaps or 'missing links' are still missing. There is a link between man and God, however. God gave to man a soul which is immortal, and a conscience to know the difference between right and wrong.

4. The DNA in every living thing contains detailed information, vital for function, growth, and reproduction. We know that information can only come from an intelligent mind, and we know that codes need intelligent inventors, and also compatible receptors. Could undirected, random processes produce the extensive, detailed genetic information in DNA? Must some mind, 'something' intelligent, not be the origin of it all?

Many people, including many scientists, believe that the 'something' is rather a Someone - almighty God who designed it, made it, and keeps it all going. They also believe that the God who created everything knows all about us and loves us in spite of our many mistakes. He loves us so much that He gave His Son, Jesus Christ, to die on a cross so that our sins could be forgiven. It is important to recognise God as our Creator, but it's even better to get to know Him as our Saviour and our heavenly Father.

3   Birds and their Beauty

The animal kingdom and the vegetable kingdom are the main divisions of the natural world, the one easy to distinguish from the other. Some people think that they both developed from the same unknown source a long time ago, but I cannot imagine that!

For most of us, birds are some of the most interesting creatures in the great animal kingdom. Wherever we are, we can admire their beauty and variety, marvel at their flying, and enjoy their singing.

British Birds

In towns and cities there are sparrows, blackbirds, starlings and robins, perhaps at a bird table in the garden. In woodlands we might see chaffinches, tree creepers, woodpeckers and owls. In the countryside there are rooks and crows, pigeons and lapwings. In the upper moorlands there are curlews and buzzards, while high in the mountains of Scotland lives the majestic golden eagle along with the hardy ptarmigan. At the coast there are umpteen different seabirds – surface-feeding gulls and ducks, divers such as the

Puffin

large sleek gannet and the smaller beautiful puffin, and long-legged waders such as redshanks, oystercatchers and herons. There is no lack of variety.

Arctic Tern

Migration brings in millions of interesting birds. Every springtime, flocks of swallows, swifts and martins make long journeys back to where they were born. The osprey comes back from Africa to its old nest site to breed once again. The Arctic Tern flies over 10,000 miles from the Antarctic and the same distance south again every autumn, never losing its way. During its lifetime this beautiful bird flies the equivalent of a trip from the earth to the moon and back! Autumn brings the sight and sound of skeins of geese flying in from the Arctic to spend the winter here, thousands of them at a time in that wide V-formation, 'honking' loudly all the way. How all these migrant birds navigate such vast distances back to exactly the same spot year on year is an unsolved puzzle. Particularly astonishing is how young birds find their way out in autumn for the first time, when maybe weeks earlier their parents have gone away without them. Migration is one of the unsolved mysteries in the natural world. No one knows exactly what the mechanism is, but it clearly works!

Migration is not confined to birds. Salmon born in an upland river bed make their way downstream to the open sea where they mature and grow for up to four years. Then they return to the selfsame section of the river where they were born, leaping up raging waterfalls, to lay their tiny eggs in the gravel beds for the next generation to repeat the cycle all over again. Thousands do this in the main Scottish rivers, but at the coast of Alaska many millions of Pacific salmon seek the rivers each autumn, providing a bounty to waiting, hungry bears. Perhaps the largest migration spectacle in the world takes place in the Serengeti grasslands of central Africa where annually around two million wildebeest surge across wide rivers full of crocodiles.

Varieties of Birds

Approximately 600 different birds have been observed in Britain, although around half of these are rare birds of passage. Our commonest bird is the tiny wren. With loud bursts of song it is more often heard than seen. There are about 19 million of them in these islands! The smallest bird is

Wren

the goldcrest, weighing the same as a 20 pence piece.[1] Our biggest bird is the sea eagle with a wing span of 2.5 metres,[2] reintroduced to Scotland about

---

[1]The American hummingbird is smaller still, some just 5 cm in size.

[2]The albatross of the Antarctic has a wing span of 3.65 metres!

30 years ago and now well established on the west coast. Among our most colourful birds are the male pheasant, the much smaller kingfisher and the blue tit. The fastest bird is the peregrine falcon, able to swoop on its prey at around 180 mph. It is in fact the fastest creature in the world!

Birds can be identified by their shapes and their colours. The male is usually more striking than the female whose more drab plumage

Peregrine Falcon

provides camouflage when sitting on a nest. Each bird also has its own distinctive song and this too can help to identify it. Some birdsong is extremely beautiful and melodious, like the blackbird's rich tones you often hear in towns, or the cadences of a skylark as it soars above grassland, also the thrush and the nightingale. Others might not be classed as tuneful - the rather flat cawing of crows and rooks, the raucous call of gulls, the busy chirping of sparrows. Of course birds do not sing for our benefit but to mark out territory or challenge intruders. Yet on a bright spring morning, it is a joy to listen to the dawn chorus from a choir of feathered singers!

Different Species

When observing birds and other living creatures, it is evident that each species maintains its boundaries, it is "true to type". For example a thrush never mates with a blackbird, or a gull with a tern, although they appear quite similar. The observed law of nature is the fixity of the species, based on their matching DNA. We do not observe the evolution of new species. What is common and well observed is adaptation within species - this is "natural selection", nature selecting within a species what survives best in certain environments. Charles Darwin observed several examples of this adaptation in the Galapagos Islands, and this led him to propose the origin and evolution of species. But evolution of new species cannot be confidently extrapolated from adaptation within species. Natural selection can explain survival by adaptation, but not the arrival of new species. The Galapagos finches were different but they were still finches, the big turtles were still turtles. Furthermore, natural selection cannot start things off when there is nothing to select from!

All this fits the Bible narrative which tells us that God made "every winged fowl after his kind" (Genesis 1.20-21), each one to fit the habitat and utilise the food supplies already there. These "kinds" (species) would adapt and change over succeeding centuries and in different isolated places to give the many sub-species we can now recognise, although doubtless some would not survive drastic climate changes. Fossils of now extinct 'prehistoric' birds demonstrate this.

Characteristics of Birds

The most obvious feature of birds is their ability to fly, intriguing to us who are held down by gravity. A dictionary defines birds as warm-blooded, egg-laying vertebrates having feathers, wings and a beak. All these features demonstrate an integrated design for birds in their place in nature.

- The ***wing of a bird*** fulfils aerodynamic design requirements, both for flapping and for gliding – it did this long before these words were thought of and used to design aeroplanes! The individual ***flight feathers*** are so structured that you would have reason to think that they too were cleverly designed: the central hollow shaft is very strong but flexible, and the side 'barbs' with smaller 'barbules' zip together to give the lightest, strongest, most efficient structure for a wing.

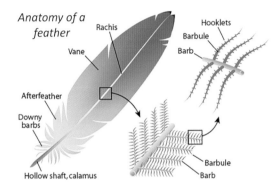

Anatomy of a feather

Rachis
Vane
Afterfeather
Downy barbs
Hollow shaft, calamus

Hooklets
Barbule
Barb
Barbule
Barb

- Reproduction involves a female bird ***laying eggs*** fertilised by its mate, each egg formed by a complex process within her body. The shell is strong

A Blackbird's eggs

enough to withstand the stresses of laying and incubation, yet weak enough for the mature chick to break out. It is porous to allow the developing chick to get oxygen and to remove its carbon dioxide. Consider too that if female birds were to carry their growing young in a womb until birth, as many other mammals do, their ability to fly and their survival would be seriously jeopardised.

- The **bones of birds** are hollow and cross-braced inside, a structure which gives maximum strength with minimum weight – just what birds need! A special example is 'shock absorber' bones in the skull of a woodpecker which prevent damage to its brain as it repeatedly slams its beak into solid wood.

- *Birds' lungs* are basically different from those of other creatures. We breathe air in and out from the top of our lungs, but in birds the air flows in at the top and out at the bottom while their blood flows through in the opposite direction. This 'counter-

Great Spotted Woodpecker

current' design gives a much better absorption of oxygen. So birds can fly fast and far, many at high altitudes where oxygen levels are reduced.

What do you think

When you observe the great variety and beauty of birds, when you listen to their songs, when you watch their easy, graceful flight - do you really think that birds evolved from dinosaurs? Do you think that the wing gradually evolved from the limb of a reptile, or feathers from the scales of a fish? What benefit to a fish would a feathery scale be, and how could a bird fly with half developed feathers?

In birds, as in many other creatures, sexual reproduction is normal and beautifully successful in producing a new generation. Gradual evolution involving partly developed male and female characteristics, ovulation, fertilisation, eggs and all, would not produce any offspring. It is obvious that everything needs to be created completely functional to begin with, made "male and female" as the Bible says.

Looking into the natural world, indeed into all the universe, purpose and design cannot be easily ignored or side-stepped, it is so obvious. Rather than believe that everything in the natural world only *appears to be* designed as you sometimes hear, just be realistic and see that it *is* designed! That it is "Undeniable".[3]

This kind of design is often called "intelligent design", but it is actually ingenious, brilliant, literally awesome – superlative adjectives cannot do it justice! The beauty of a bird, the structure of a feather, of an egg, the function of its millions of tiny cells, its DNA – all clearly and logically point to an all-wise Designer and an Almighty Creator. Why not follow the evidence where it leads, as many others have done?[4]

---

[3]*Undeniable: How Biology confirms our Intuition that Life is designed*, Douglas Axe, HarperCollins 2016

[4] *There is a God: How the world's most notorious atheist changed his mind,* Anthony Flew, HarperCollins 2007

4 Plants and their Necessity

The atoms and molecules that are part of us and of everything else are so small that we cannot see them. We need specialised apparatus and the methods of physics and chemistry to reveal them. But for now, just open your eyes and see the beauty of nature, for it is everywhere! You don't need to go far, but the more you look, the more of it you will be able to enjoy.

Birds are fascinating and many are beautiful, but they usually fly away too quickly for us to observe them properly. But in the gardens, in the fields and in the forests, we can inspect other living things at close range. We can touch flowers and smell them, take some indoors to enjoy them. Look at a snowdrop, a daffodil, or a lily; smell a rose or a hyacinth, even dissect them and examine the perfection of their fine structure! No two are exactly the same! Huge variety and natural beauty are to be found everywhere.

As the seasons change, beauty unfolds in the great panoramas of our landscapes. Watch the fresh summer greens develop, and later fade to yellows, then to deepening gold and bronze. The gigantic, remote planets and stars have their own interest, but they are lifeless spheres of rocks or hot gasses. Here beside us are living things - growing flowers, grasses and trees; mobile birds, animals and insects; nature teeming with life, that amazing characteristic which we ourselves possess and value more than anything else – life! Where did it all come from? Was it all accidental, or was it intentional?

Flowers

We enjoy flowers because of their colour and texture, and often their fragrance too.[1] Whether it is the wild flower meadow or the herbaceous border, the rose garden or the parkland, the tiny blue forget-me-not or the giant yellow sunflower, the prolific summer-long daisy or the equally prolific but short lived cherry blossom - all bring cheer and pleasure. And of course there is the charm of cut flowers and flower arrangements: a simple way

to bring a smile to someone's face, an easy way to show appreciation and emotion.

What would you suggest is the flower of the month as the year progresses? – start with the snowdrop, the crocus, the daffodil and then what would you choose? - all year round variety and beauty for us to enjoy and appreciate!

---

[1]Their smell is really to attract pollinating insects.

Forests

Trees make up about a quarter of all plant life, and there may be around 100,000 different kinds of trees in the world. In the UK there are nearly 4,000 million trees growing just now, with over half of them in Scotland. Trees are an important source of building material and fuel, often over-exploited, and many provide our fruits in their season.. They also provide a habitat for countless creatures large and small, and they have a vital role in soaking up much of the carbon dioxide which we produce in excess.

In addition to their usefulness, trees have a striking beauty. Look at a mature oak or an elm, or a Scots pine on a heather-clad hillside – each a sculpture shaped by wind and weather. Walk in a woodland or a forest, look up to the treetops or along the avenues and leave behind the stresses of daily life. Wonder at the seasonal changes as deciduous trees like oak, silver birch, beech, lose their leaves in autumn, after treating us to such a rich tapestry of glorious changing colours, then clothe themselves again in every shade of green each springtime. In contrast, the evergreens with their sharp needles keep their

colour all year round, and sometimes delight us with the silent beauty of their branches crusted with frost or laden with snow on a hard winter's day.

Food Supplies

As well as being plentiful and beautiful, plants are our most fundamental food source, and upon it the nourishment of many other creatures depends.[2] Most of us eat several varieties of vegetables and fruits, local and imported, colourful and nutritious, in addition to the staples like potatoes, rice and bread.

The commonest plants that grow everywhere are the grasses. We cannot digest the cellulose which they contain, but grazing animals (herbivores) can do this. Many of these provide meat for us when they are butchered, as they do for predator carnivores in the wild. The energy we get from eating meat is derived from what was stored in the plants which the animals digested. This in turn came from the sun by a marvellous process called photosynthesis.

Photosynthesis

Photosynthesis occurs within the plant cells which make up their structure. As you can see in Figure 4, these cells are rectangular with a rigid outer wall. This is made of cellulose and encloses all the components required for growth and replication according to the DNA information in the nucleus.[3] The **chloroplast** in the cell is where this photosynthesis happens, making the cellulose and everything else the plants need. Thus they produce their own food and support their own weight - that is, they "grow".

---

[2]According to Genesis 1, God made edible vegetation – grass, herbs, trees with their seeds in place (v.11-12), before He made the land animals (v.24-25) which would need this food supply, as would mankind also (v.29-30).

[3]Compare animal cells described earlier.

PLANT CELL

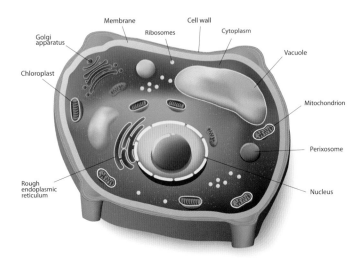

Photosynthesis starts with water and carbon dioxide. Water is absorbed through the roots, and carbon dioxide is absorbed through pores in the leaves and tissues. The sun's energy then drives a chemical reaction in the chloroplast to turn the carbon dioxide and water into carbohydrates like glucose, sugar, starch and cellulose. At the same time oxygen is produced and released into the atmosphere. Animals use up oxygen and release carbon dioxide by respiration, plants do the reverse, using up carbon dioxide and releasing oxygen by photosynthesis. It looks like a perfectly designed system, all wonderfully balanced, worldwide in scope, but sadly becoming unbalanced due to human activities.

The green colour of plants is due to a unique substance called **chlorophyll** which is the catalyst to make photosynthesis occur in the chloroplast. Its molecule absorbs the red-orange and blue-violet parts of the sunlight spectrum, leaving the green colour for us to see. As chlorophyll absorbs this energy from the sun, its electrons are given the ability to "reduce"

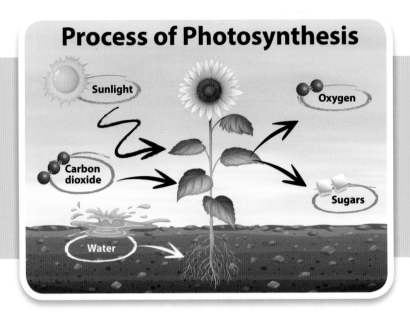

Process of Photosynthesis

Sunlight

Oxygen

Carbon dioxide

Sugars

Water

the carbon dioxide so that it can become "hydrated" and thus make carbohydrates, and at the same time release oxygen.

The chlorophyll molecule has a very interesting and unique structure, clearly designed for a special purpose. An unusual metal atom, **magnesium,** is held in place by four nitrogen atoms, and embedded in folded carbon-based polymer chains. This arrangement of atoms enables the sun's energy to energise the electrons which change carbon dioxide and water into carbohydrates and oxygen. In some ways, chlorophyll can be thought of as the counterpart in plants, of the haemoglobin in the blood of animals. Haemoglobin transports oxygen by means of a special design of four iron atoms embedded in a huge molecule made up of convoluted carbon-based chains. [4]

---

[4]Chlorophyll has the chemical formula $C_{55}H_{72}N_4O_5Mg$, haemoglobin is (approx) $C_{2932}H_{4724}N_{828}O_{840}S_8Fe_4$

What do you think

In all of nature, especially in living things, design is stamped on whole organisms like birds and flowers, and on all their unique molecular components like haemoglobin and chlorophyll. How could these develop blindly a little bit at a time and find their place with others in a complex cell? How could gradual change in an organism "improve a species" as Darwinian evolution requires? Partly formed organs are no use and incomplete organisms will not survive! Partly formed or incomplete cells are not viable!

You cannot really get past the fact that "intelligent design" is to be seen everywhere. Does the intricacy and beauty of everything not make you wonder about an intelligent Designer and Creator?

As for the beauty of it all, the Bible says that in the beginning God saw that everything He made was good, yes very good (Genesis 1.31). Although it has doubtless diminished over time, that beauty lingers wherever you look. God could have made everything in dull grey monochrome, but He didn't, for He loves beauty. He made it as it is, in such a rich palette of blending colours. And He made us as we are, with the ability to examine, explore, look and learn - to enjoy all these varied colours, shapes, sounds, smells and feelings - the beauty of it all! Humans can appreciate beauty as no other creature can.

Long ago someone said, "O LORD how manifold are Thy works; in wisdom hast Thou made them all: the earth is full of Thy riches" (Psalm 104.24). Could you join in? It makes excellent sense, and it is supported by science!

5 Insects and their Society

What do you think about insects? We can be fascinated and charmed by the many beautiful things all around us, the birds and beasts, the flowers and forests. But insects? - those busy little creatures you find everywhere? What about ants, bees, wasps, spiders, grasshoppers, ladybirds, butterflies, dragonflies, and so on?

Insects may not be near the top of our list of interests or even included in the things we admire. They are not our favourites! Sweep them out; kill them off rather! Yes, for many are responsible for the spread of infection. Mosquitoes are responsible for malaria, one of the world's worst killers. Midges in the west of Scotland are a legendary nuisance!

But balance this with the role of the honey bee, responsible for the pollination of so many of our crops. And spiders, efficient predators which keep the numbers of flies in check (including these mosquitoes in Africa and elsewhere). Then there are butterflies and dragonflies in all their bright colours, and ladybirds too which devour the aphids which spoil many garden plants. And do not forget the role of insects in the great balanced ecosystem of nature. They are an abundant and nutritious food supply for huge numbers of birds – swifts and swallows gulp down millions of them as they swoop through the air; nesting birds in our woodlands and gardens depend on them to rear their chicks successfully. In our rivers, many fish eat insects on the surface, and of course anglers exploit this.

Watch out for Ants

When you see ants, they are always scurrying about - gathering food or transporting their eggs or nesting materials one piece at a time. Sometimes you will see a few of them working together to move objects larger than themselves. Ants display the highest level of organisation found in an animal society, with clearly defined roles and division of labour for defence, food gathering, building and reproduction. They function as a huge co-operating team, without supervision or direction from managers. They communicate by scent, touch and sound. Totally unselfish, each one has the common aim of benefitting the whole colony, and the production and protection of the next generation.

The common wood ant in the UK builds up a huge anthill from numerous small items of vegetation. Such anthills, up to a metre in diameter and height, can be seen in many of our woodlands. Beneath the surface of an anthill is a labyrinth of passageways kept ventilated and clean, suitable for protecting and nourishing offspring while insulating them from the cold to come.

They gather and store their food in the summer from a variety of sources, or else they will perish in the winter. These busy creatures use every opportunity while they can! The Bible notes how they operate without "guide, overseer, or ruler" and refers to them as an example we humans should follow (Proverbs 6.5-8). It also says that they are "not strong" but they are "exceeding wise" (Proverbs 30.24-25). Their bodies are small and their brains are tiny. Do you think this wisdom, this social instinct embedded in their DNA for them to survive, evolved over billions of years from something else, from something dead? Or was it endowed by their Creator at the beginning for them to fit into the ecosystem?

For the record, ants are among the most numerous species on earth. It is claimed that if they were all gathered together they would weigh more than all the vertebrate animals on earth! There are over 20,000 species of ants and they are found everywhere except Antarctica, Greenland and Iceland. Of all the species, the most fearsome is the tropical Army Ant. A colony may have over 15 million workers and once on the march they cannot be stopped. They can consume up to 500,000 prey items per day! When necessary, the first ones link together to form a living bridge over a gap and the rest of the colony crosses over them. They do not build a nest like other ant species. Rather they bind together into a living nest in a hollow tree or burrow, holding on to each other's legs to make a 'bivouac' with all the necessary substructure inside. More co-operation and embedded wisdom! Amazing ants!

Beware of Bees

Turning to bees, many people will think of honey and hives, a good reason why we might be interested in them. On the down side, we know that they can give a painful sting, but their characteristic hum is a beautiful summer sound, not produced vocally but by their two pairs of tiny wings which beat around 200 times per second! There are at least 20,000 species of bees in the world. In the UK, wild bumblebees and smaller solitary bees are quite common, but the honey bee is probably of most interest to us. They are beautiful creatures, and have an organised colony structure at least as complex as that of ants.

Bees have five eyes, three simple ones on top of their heads and two compound ones at the side. They discern colours as we do, but they are more sensitive to ultra-violet which helps them to find flowers from which they gather nectar and pollen. It is collected on special parts of their hind legs, and as these 'busy bees' fly from flower to flower they perform the vital function of pollination on which the reproduction of many plants depends.[1] Pollen is their main food source, and it is from nectar that they produce honey – more than they need for the nourishment of their next generation and harvested all over the world for human use. Honey is stored in the honeycomb, in beautiful hexagonal cells made of beeswax – another commodity harvested because of its usefulness.

---

[1] Insect pollination for food production has been valued at £134 billion per annum, with most of it done by bees.

Bee 'society' is fully organised. Each colony or hive has one queen bee – a larger female responsible for laying fertilised eggs, up to 2,500 per day in the summer! The eggs go into separate cells of the honeycomb where they will develop into larvae then hatch into tiny bees. The hive is sustained by an army of 'workers', sterile females which go off to harvest pollen and nectar. These are the bees we see around, the ones that sting. The stinger is barbed, so that once sunk into the victim it detaches along with a tiny sac of venom and the bee dies. Workers also keep the hive clean, removing dead material and circulating the air by beating their wings.

Returning with pollen they communicate with others by performing a 'figure of eight' dance at the hive with its direction and duration giving the direction and distance of a discovered food source. How do you explain this fascinating method of communication? Who taught the bee to dance with such a purpose? In winter, workers form a cluster round the queen to keep her warm, taking turns to be at the outside so that no bee gets too cold. There are also drones, males which mate with a new queen and then die, or are killed off as winter comes. A queen bee can live up to five years, and when it dies, workers create a new queen by selecting a newly hatched larva and feeding it on 'royal jelly', a special substance prepared and ready when required. Bees are amazing too!

Now that we've described ants and bees, you might want to research spiders and their beautiful webs, spotted red ladybirds and how they control aphids, butterflies and their colourful, fragile wings, dragonflies with their dainty form and compound eyes. There's a lot more! Studying insects is called entomology.

What do you think ?

Wherever you look among the insect population, it's not only numbers that impress (or annoy) you. It is the way that they depend on each other, and on other living things, and how other living things depend on them. They are a necessary part of some of the great integrated cycles of nature. Maybe you need to ask if and how the different parts could evolve separately to be available for each other, bees for the flowers and flowers for the bees, for example. How did each organism survive and progress without the other ones there at the same time, to do their bit for each other?

Or do you see this cycle as a whole, created 'up and running' with all the interlocking, complex cogs of the great wheel (or wheels) in place to begin with? Then rather than call it 'nature' and try to fit evolution and natural selection to it, could you not call it 'creation' and be amazed at it all - the work of an almighty and all-wise Creator? Many scientists and others all over the world believe that this is the best way to understand it.

Do you think it was all accidental, or intentional?

6 The Sea and its Bounty

About 70% of the surface of the earth is covered by water. Fresh water in rivers and lakes is constantly replenished by snow, rain and mist, but most fresh water is locked up in glaciers and in the icecaps. The sea contains 97% of the water on Earth, definitely not drinking water! It contains over 3% sodium chloride by weight. Its most abundant ions are chloride 1.9%, sodium 1.06%, sulphate 0.26%, magnesium 0.13%, calcium 0.040%, potassium 0.038%, bicarbonate 0.014%, bromide 0.007%, and there are many others.

The deepest part of the sea is the Marianas Trench in the western Pacific Ocean. It is nearly 7 miles deep, more than a mile greater than the height of Mount Everest. The huge amount of water on Earth smoothes out the heating effect of the sun and moderates the world's climate due to the large heat capacity of water. It also dissolves carbon dioxide, removing more of it from the atmosphere than the forests do.

The sea is fascinating, especially to those who can access it readily. The shoreline is beautiful, the shallows inviting to swim in (sometimes!), the intertidal region full of variety and interest. The deeper sea stretching to the far horizon has long invited exploration and travel to distant lands, and has beckoned fishermen to venture farther and farther from the shore. What they have pulled out of the sea has often been surprising! What sailors have seen in its different moods is unforgettable, from mirror calm, trapping sailing ships, to angry storms threatening the most powerful of modern vessels. Even for observers on dry land, huge waves crashing on a rocky shore is awe-inspiring, potentially dangerous too.

Sea-life

The seas are teeming with life, creatures of all shapes and sizes, from tiny invisible plankton to the great whales. The amount and variety of living things in the seas is staggering.[1] The most abundant life-form is this **plankton** which drifts in the currents. It is the primary food source for all sea creatures.

The first part of this food chain is **phytoplankton,** plant based material which, like all plants, grows by photosynthesis. In this phytoplankton, sunlight converts carbon dioxide and water into sugars and oxygen, helped by phosphate and nitrate in the water. Most of the photosynthesis on earth takes place in the

---

[1]Abundance and variety in the seas were built into creation at the beginning. Genesis 1.20-22: "Let the waters bring forth abundantly the moving creature that has life."

oceans rather than on land, and this also produces much of the oxygen in the air we breathe. **Zooplankton**, or animal plankton, feeds on phytoplankton. It exists at all depths whereas phytoplankton keeps near the surface to benefit from sunlight. Zooplankton consists mainly of tiny or undeveloped fish larvae and crustaceans which all other sea creatures then feed upon.

There are over 30,000 different species of **fish**, most of them in the Pacific Ocean. In the seas around the British Isles there may be around 200 species. The familiar ones are cod and haddock; sole, plaice and skate; salmon, trout, mackerel and herring. Herring are the second most plentiful fish in the sea, moving in huge shoals which come to the surface to feed. They are the most efficient converters of plankton into human food. The most plentiful fish is the bristlemouth, but we never meet it because it lives at depths of over 1000 ft. It is estimated that there are trillions of them!

Fish are evidently suited to their habitat, most of them beautifully streamlined for swimming and with a strong tail for propulsion. For reproduction, females lay eggs (spawn) which are then fertilised by the males of the same species, not another one that might be passing. Time and again we note the boundaries of species are not crossed, even related ones. Fish spawn contains millions of eggs[2] - any excess contributes to the zooplankton.

---

[2]Contrast this with birds which lay only a few already fertilised eggs.

The oxygen content of water is critical for the survival of all aquatic creatures. How fish breathe is necessarily linked to and designed for their environment. Our lungs absorb oxygen from air, but a fish absorbs oxygen in gills tucked in behind its head from the water which flows into its mouth and out over them. These gills are red or pink comb-like structures with filaments extending outwards, each having many branches called primary lamellae. These in turn have many tiny, thin-walled, secondary lamellae giving a large surface area to absorb oxygen into the fish's blood and also remove carbon dioxide from it. Gills absorb oxygen much more efficiently than our lungs do, in keeping with the fact that the concentration of dissolved oxygen in water is much less than it is in air. Whilst gills and lungs both absorb oxygen, their different structures show design for different environments. Lungs did not (could not) gradually evolve from gills! Creatures with lungs soon drown in water. Creatures with gills soon drown in air!

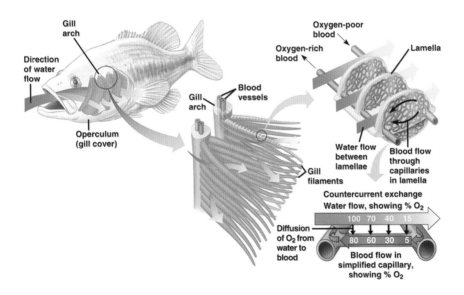

Shellfish

Shellfish production is a large and profitable industry in many countries. Molluscs like mussels, clams (scallops) and oysters anchor themselves to surfaces and filter plankton out of the water. Crustaceans like lobsters, crabs and prawns live and move on the sea floor, feeding on smaller creatures. Like fish they breathe by means of gills, but shellfish are not fish. Fish are vertebrates (have backbones) and swim. Shellfish are invertebrates with hard shells (exoskeletons) which they renew (moult) to allow for their growth.

The lobster is a popular but unusual shellfish, caught in baited traps ('pots' or 'creels') mostly in coastal waters. On cooking, it changes colour from a beautiful blue which is good camouflage on the sea floor, to a vivid red. It has massive claws, long antennae, and protruding eyes. These are compound eyes with large numbers of photoreceptors, using mirrors rather than lenses to focus multiple images. Such eyes have a very wide angle view and are better at detecting fast movement in low light conditions. Lobsters, one of the many "wonders in the deep", can live up to 30 years when they might weigh around 15 kg.

Lobsters and some other sea creatures such as octopuses have blue blood. This contains haemocyanin, a protein containing copper atoms, whereas mammals have red blood based on haemoglobin which contains iron atoms. At lower temperatures, haemocyanin transports oxygen better than haemoglobin. You can easily see how each kind of creature has exactly what it needs for the different environments.

Whales

There are seven types of whales, of which the blue whale is the largest mammal known. It can live for about 80 years and at maturity can be over 100 ft long and weigh around 200 tons[3] (the African elephant is the biggest land animal, weighing 'only' about 7 tons). A baby whale drinks over 80 gallons of its mother's milk every day. These whales feed exclusively on huge amounts of tiny Antarctic Krill which they filter out of the water through baleen at the sides of their mouths. They can swim underwater for up to 10 minutes and breathe air through blowholes (like nostrils) on top of their heads. Whales were hunted to the verge of extinction for over 100 years but numbers are now recovering although the blue whale population is less than 1% of what it once was.

---

[3]This is much bigger than the biggest dinosaur which has been described from fossil remains.

Many other mammals such as seals, dolphins, and porpoises live in and on the sea, along with millions of sea birds which like them depend on the abundance of food in the sea. Under the sea, plant life ('seaweed') thrives, including vast underwater 'forests' of large brown kelp which was once harvested for iodine and potash production, and is still used as a source of alginate.

The resources of the sea have benefitted mankind for a long time, but sad to say, greed and carelessness have exploited these resources and now there are real scarcities in some areas. Industrial societies have seriously polluted parts of the sea and now plastic waste is an increasing problem. Atmospheric pollution, global warming and associated climate change are also threatening the health of the sea and the land. Does this concern you?

What do you think (**?**)━━

Photosynthesis by plants in the sea and on the land uses up carbon dioxide and produces oxygen, whilst animals in the sea and on the land use up oxygen and produce carbon dioxide. Part of a large-scale, balanced plan?

The sea contains such a variety of creatures – plants and animals, vertibrates and invertibrates, crustaceans and molluscs. The variety of creatures on land and in the air is also huge – all gradually evolved from hypothetical ancestors, or each kind specially created?

The gills and scales of fish are quite different from the lungs and feathers of birds, and from the lungs, skin and hair of mammals. Evolved, or each deliberately designed for its place in nature?

Haemocyanin with copper atoms is in the blue blood of many crustaceans but haemoglobin with iron atoms is in the red blood of animals. If they all gradually evolved, these protein molecules would have needed some unusual chemistry and some strange coincidences to select these different metal atoms randomly, and incorporate them correctly into the appropriate places. Partly formed, nothing would work to keep the oxygen flowing! Is it not more like foresight and design that got it right to begin with?

7

The Universe and its Immensity

Living cells are incredibly complex. Atoms and molecules are incredibly small. Now let's go to astronomy and consider things that are incredibly big, almost too big to comprehend. The measurements are so large that a special unit is used - the *light-year*, the almost unimaginable distance of 5,880,000,000,000 miles,[1] about 63,000 times the distance between the earth and the sun.

On a clear, dark night and away from the glow of towns and cities, the stars appear much clearer. An awe-inspiring vastness stretches out across the sky. The wonder of it is timeless, although predictions and theories now dominate astronomy. Like other branches of science, it has developed greatly in the last two centuries, but ancient records left by Assyrian, Babylonian, Chinese, and Arabian peoples are valued today to compare with recent observations.

The Solar System

Planet Earth moves round the sun in its year-long orbit as part of the solar system. The sun is classified as a medium sized yellow star, diameter about 865,000 miles, 109 times the diameter of the earth, 745 times the mass of

---

[1] A light-year is the distance light travels in a year's time (186,398 miles per second x no of seconds in a year).

all the planets put together. Over a million earths could fit inside it! Energy is generated in its interior by hydrogen atoms combining to form helium atoms at a temperature of around 15,000,000 °C. Its surface temperature is about 5,500 °C. At a distance of 93,000,000 miles from the sun, Earth receives the correct amount of radiation from this correct size of star to give the correct temperatures we can live with - all beautifully matched! If the sun were hotter, or if Earth were nearer it, all life would burn up. If it were cooler, or Earth farther away, all would freeze to death.

Eight major planets move round the sun in an anticlockwise direction, each anchored to it by gravitation, while each also spins on its own axis. There are four inner planets - Mercury, Venus, Earth and Mars, relatively small, dense and rocky; and four outer ones, Jupiter, Saturn, Uranus and Neptune, which are huge spheres of gaseous material. Venus is often seen bright in the east before sunrise and in the west just after sunset - it is the 'morning star' and the 'evening star', always near the sun. At night, Jupiter can be seen higher in the sky and brighter than the stars around it. It has four moons which a basic telescope can pick out. The other planets are less easy to locate without some guidance.

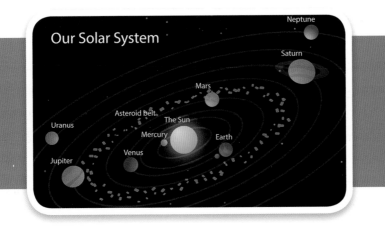

Planets move in elliptical orbits ('squashed circles'). Mercury nearest the sun has a very elongated ellipse, but the earth's orbit is almost circular. If it were elongated, then for some of the year, Earth would be nearer the sun and get very much hotter, then get very much colder when it was further away. Planets closer to the sun orbit round it faster - a year on Mercury is about a quarter of our year (its 'day' lasts for 58 of our days due to slower spin on its axis). Planets farther away orbit the sun more slowly - Neptune's year is 165 of our years (its 'day' is 16.1 hours due to a faster spin on its axis). The length of year and the length of day on Earth enable life to thrive. If our 'day' were much longer than 24 hours, extremely cold nights and extremely hot days would develop. If it were shorter, weather patterns would be unstable and the gases of the atmosphere would spin off into space. Also, because the earth's axis is not at right angles to the sun's rays but tilted by 23.5 degrees, the energy influx spreads over a wider area north and south of the equator. Seasons are thus extended, and the very hot and the very cold regions of the earth are minimised. All these factors combine to make Earth an appropriate and safe home for living things. Was all this just a cosmic accident?

The Constellations

Constellations are groups of stars, first recognised by the ancients and given names mostly after figures in Greek mythology. Ptolemy (150 AD) compiled a list of forty-eight. Now eighty-eight constellations are recognised to map out regions of the sky. For us, looking north, the Plough or Great Dipper, lies well above the horizon. Two of its stars point up to the north pole star, Polaris,[2] a yellow supergiant about 650 light-years away, 37 times bigger

---

[2]This and other fixed stars were used historically for navigational purposes.

than the sun. Looking south, Orion is a clear constellation which moves higher in the sky as winter progresses, recognised usually by the three stars making up its 'belt'. Following the direction of these stars down to the left leads to the brightest star we can see from the UK, a greenish twinkling star called Sirius. It is 8.7 light-years distant, and is actually 26 times as bright as the sun. But the sun *appears* much brighter since it is only 8.3 'light-*minutes*' distant.

Two stars in Orion are noteworthy: Betelguese at the top left 'shoulder', and Rigel at the bottom right 'foot'. Betelguese is one of the largest stars known. It is a red supergiant, 430 light-years distant. If it were placed where our sun is, the inner half of the solar system out beyond Jupiter would fit inside it! Can you imagine that? Rigel is a good bit smaller but it is the brightest star in Orion. It is a blue-white supergiant, about 80 times bigger than the sun, 1050 light-years distant. Those different colours are due to different surface temperatures, varying between 3,000 °C (red dwarfs) and 40,000 °C (blue-white giants).

Some constellations make up the twelve 'signs of the Zodiac' which are used to describe where the sun appears to be during each of the twelve months of Earth's orbit. A superstitious, pagan system called astrology is based on them but it is totally misleading. Most of the names of the constellations are strange to us, and anyway you need a lot of imagination to see how the star patterns match these names!

The Stars

Nobody knows how many stars there are! It is said that with the naked eye, about 3,000 stars could be counted in one hemisphere, meaning that around 6,000 stars could be visible from Earth. In 1610 Galileo made the first telescope and was able to see ten times more. As telescopes improved in power and resolution, the number kept increasing to over 600,000 in the1850s. Now with the advent of radio astronomy the number is literally uncountable![3]

No two stars are identical. They have different colours, brightnesses, sizes, temperatures, speeds of rotation, compositions, and distances from Earth. The nearest star is alpha Centauri, not seen in the northern hemisphere (it is one of the 'pointers' to the Southern Cross). It is 4.3 light-years distant, and is the third brightest star seen from Earth. A bright one in the northern

---

[3]That is exactly what the Bible said long ago! "The host of heaven cannot be numbered" (Jeremiah 33.22).

sky is Arcturus, 37 light-years distant, 12.5 times bigger than the sun, while eta Carinae is 4 million times as bright as the sun and over 100 times more massive, but at 6,400 light-years distant it is not even visible to the naked eye! One of the largest ones known is VY Canis Majoris in the Milky Way, near Sirius, a 'red hyper-giant', 3,900 light-years distant, 1420 times the size of the sun, much bigger than Betelguese mentioned above! The smallest star recognised is a white dwarf, half the size of the moon, at 100 light-years distance.

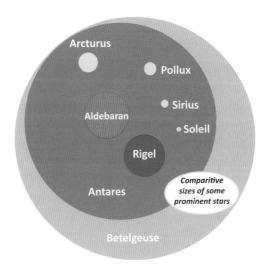

The Vastness of Space

The solar system is located in the Milky Way galaxy which is around 100,000 light-years in diameter. Sometimes on a clear night you can see it stretching right across the sky. It contains over 200 thousand million stars! With the naked eye three more galaxies can just be seen, the two Clouds of Magellan and the Andromeda Galaxy apparently 2.25 million light-years distant. There may be over 100 million swirling galaxies, perhaps billions of light-years distant, and we are told that the universe is still expanding! These sizes and distances are really too huge to visualise or imagine, as is the vastness of empty space. In fact, it is now readily admitted that the structure and dimensions of the universe are beyond human comprehension.

One thing has become clear. The huge universe is fine-tuned, just as the tiny atom is. The universe, and our place in it, is what it is because the fundamental physical constants which define space have very precise values, for example the gravitational force. If they were even slightly different, the universe would be very different, earth would not exist, the necessary conditions for life would not exist either. One author called this the Goldilocks Enigma[4] – it is "just right". Another said it would appear that the universe knew we were coming!

What do you think

In the face of such vastness, such numbers of stars, do you get the feeling that Earth is just a small insignificant planet in one of many huge galaxies? And does this mean that man who lives on it is more insignificant still? Far from it! It has been said that the most wonderful thing about astronomy is the astronomer.

Stars are lifeless, sterile. Man has life and intelligence, the unique ability to explore and to appreciate something of the grandeur of the universe, and from it to learn of the power and glory of its Creator who is also our Creator. He wants us to get to know Him. He gave us a soul and a conscience, and a Bible to read. His Son came here to Earth among us to show God's great love for us by dying for our sins so that we could be forgiven.

---

[4]*The Goldilocks Enigma: Why is the Universe just right for Life?* Paul Davies, 2007

If the universe is so great, how much greater must be its Creator! The starry skies are like a huge billboard with a message which no one can erase, which everyone can read, proclaiming God! A verse in the Bible says that God's eternal power and wisdom can be seen in all creation, so that we are without an excuse if we ignore Him (Romans 1.18).

You owe it to yourself to examine the evidence and consider Creation!

Ten things you're NOT often told!

1. Evolution of species is NOT a fact.

    It is a theory or hypothesis extended (extrapolated) from observing how living things adapt to changing conditions. Many proposals and assumptions are then built in without good evidence. Adaptation within a species is much different from evolution into new species.

2. Evolution is NOT probable (likely to happen) nor reasonable (making good sense).

    The odds against it are huge. Everyday experience and common sense requires that everything we encounter has a cause, a designer, and a maker.

3. Energy (which fills the universe) can NOT be created by nothing and from nothing.

    The *first law of thermodynamics* tells us this - NO exceptions exist in the real world. A big problem is being overlooked when we're told that something came from nothing.

4. Complex structures do NOT by themselves come from simpler ones.

    The *second law of thermodynamics* tells us this - with NO exceptions. This law (and all our experience) says that complex structures (e.g. protein molecules, cells) rather break down into simpler ones by themselves. Chaos or disorder (entropy) increases in systems when left to themselves. To arrange order or provide information, some external intelligence or mechanism is always necessary.

5. Life does NOT come from non-living matter.
    This is the *law of biogenesis* – NO exceptions in the real world.

6. Mutations within living cells do NOT provide a feasible route to "improved" species.
    As DNA copies, accidental changes are resisted; any that continue are nearly always harmful to the organism.

7. Evolution is NOT supported by the fossil record.
    There are NO simple fossils at 'start'; and NO 'link' fossils 'between'. The fossil record supports a huge flood model much better - fossils of creatures buried in ecological zones, then disturbed by volcanic action and movements of the earth's crust.

8. It is NOT certain that the world is thousands of millions of years old. This age is calculated by making some assumptions about certain processes such as radioactive decay. These assumptions are unlikely to be true. Other calculations come up with very much shorter time scales.

9. Many scientists do NOT believe in evolution.
    Among them are some who have no religious faith or a belief in God, and have gone on record to state that the theory is faulty. Others have freely admitted its weakness and noted its problems, yet cling to it!

10. People believe in evolution mainly because they DO NOT want God. Evolution conveniently removes the prospect of accountability to God, and allows any kind of lifestyle.

A Final Consideration!

- Some people say they don't believe what they used to believe, maybe "brain-washed"?
- Others think it's important to look good in front of others – maybe "white-washed"?
- And some say that they have been "blood-washed", taking a verse from the Bible for this.

Which group do you belong to?

Brain-washed?

Have educational systems and so much media coverage brain-washed you into believing that this beautiful world and every wonderful thing in it was not created by God, but that it all gradually evolved from nothing over a long, long time? Perhaps in early life you did think that God created everything!

In this book I've tried to show that evolution does not match the evidence. In everyday life we know that everything has a maker and a designer. What you are reading now didn't just happen or evolve by itself - someone planned it, wrote it, and printed it! How can you believe that this is not true of everything around you - from the marvel of life and the coded information in DNA to the majesty of the universe? Did it all just happen by chance?

Have you also been brain-washed to believe that there is nothing after death? In your serious moments you know that this cannot be true either, there is so much evidence the other way. Remember that no amount of brain-washing or even wishful thinking will alter the facts of the matter. It won't change what the Bible says – *"After death, the judgement"* (Hebrews 9.27).

White-washed?

No matter what we believe, we often have to recognise our own mistakes and failures. But we like to appear respectable, and so we put on a good face. Or we hope that the good we do will somehow cancel out the bad we've done. We try a white-wash!

The problem with white-wash is that it does not change anything inside - where it matters. It also wears off easily! In fact, people usually see through it!

White-wash does not deceive God. The Bible says that *"man looks on the outward appearance, but God looks on the heart"* (1 Samuel 16.7). He knows what we really are, not what others think we are, or even what **we** think we are. He wants us to be honest about our sin, to face up to it and then get rid of it. God says, *"He that covers his sins shall not prosper; but whoever confesses and forsakes them shall have mercy"* (Proverbs 28.13).

Blood-washed?

There is only one thing which can remove our sin, and the guilt and misery that goes with it. The Bible says, *"The blood of Jesus Christ, God's Son, cleanses us from all sin"* (1 John1.7).

God could not simply ignore our sins or excuse them, because He is holy and just. So He gave His Son to bear the judgement of our sin. The blood of Christ, shed on the cross, is the token of the price paid and the penalty borne for our sins so that we could be forgiven.

To benefit from what Christ has done, you must put your trust in Him. Aware of your sinfulness, turn in faith to Jesus Christ and accept Him as your own Saviour. When you do that, you will find for yourself that His blood cleanses you from all your sin.